SEASONS

Spring

by Ann Herriges

BELLWETHER MEDIA • MINNEAPOLIS, MN

Note to Librarians, Teachers, and Parents:

Blastoff! Readers are carefully developed by literacy experts and combine standards-based content with developmentally appropriate text.

Level 1 provides the most support through repetition of high-frequency words, light text, predictable sentence patterns, and strong visual support.

Level 2 offers early readers a bit more challenge through varied simple sentences, increased text load, and less repetition of high-frequency words.

Level 3 advances early-fluent readers toward fluency through increased text and concept load, less reliance on visuals, longer sentences, and more literary language.

Whichever book is right for your reader, Blastoff! Readers are the perfect books to build confidence and encourage a love of reading that will last a lifetime!

This edition first published in 2007 by Bellwether Media.

No part of this publication may be reproduced in whole or in part without written permission of the publisher. For information regarding permission, write to Bellwether Media Inc., Attention: Permissions Department, Post Office Box 1C, Minnetonka, MN 55345-9998.

Library of Congress Cataloging-in-Publication Data
Herriges, Ann.
  Spring / by Ann Herriges.
    p. cm. – (Seasons) (Blastoff! readers)
Summary: "Simple text and supportive images introduce beginning readers to the characteristics of the season of spring. Intended for students in kindergarten through third grade."
  Includes bibliographical references and index.
  ISBN-10: 1-60014-031-9 (hardcover : alk. paper)
  ISBN-13: 978-1-60014-031-0 (hardcover : alk. paper)
  1. Spring—Juvenile literature. I. Title. II. Series.

  QB637.5.H47 2007
  508.2–dc22   2006000612

Text copyright © 2007 by Bellwether Media.
Printed in the United States of America.

Table of Contents

What Is Spring?	4
Plants in Spring	10
Animals in Spring	14
People in Spring	20
Glossary	22
To Learn More	23
Index	24

Spring is one of Earth's four **seasons**. Spring comes after winter.

During spring the
sun rises earlier
and sets later.

Each day the sun climbs higher
in the sky and warms the air.

Sunshine melts the snow. Water drips from icicles. Ice melts on lakes and ponds.

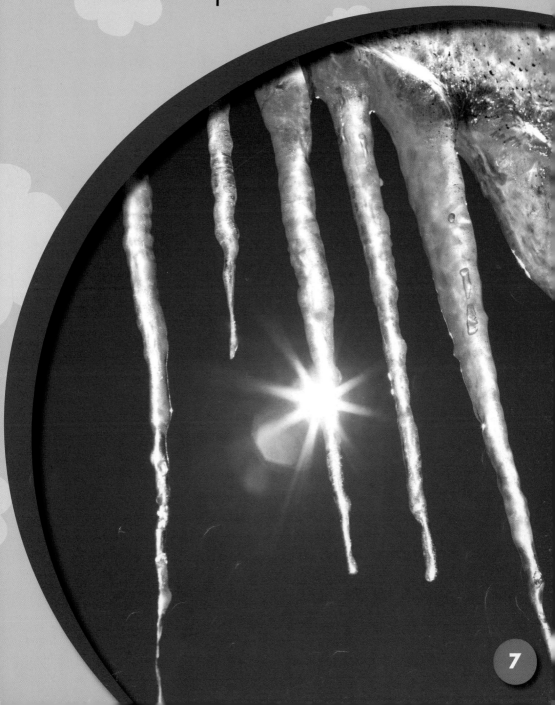

Strong winds blow
thunderstorms across
the sky in spring.

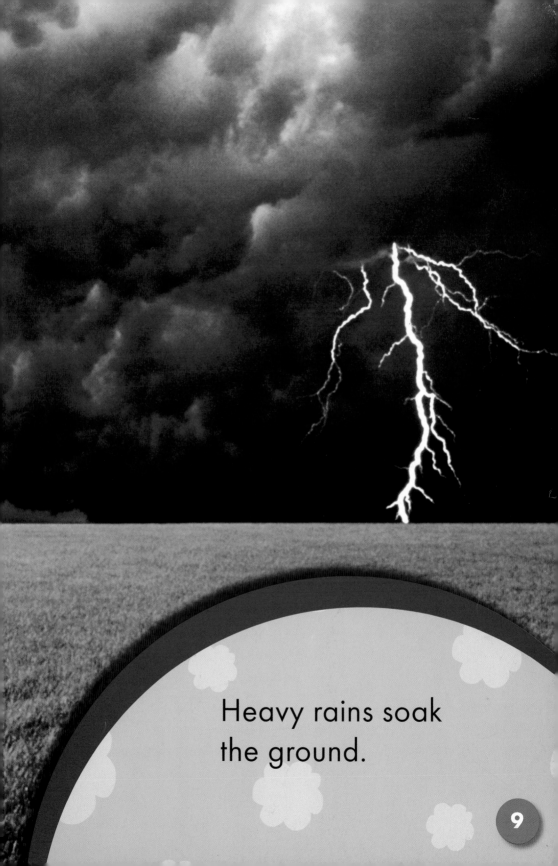

Heavy rains soak
the ground.

Sunshine and rain help plants grow. Buds grow on trees and then open into leaves.

Grass changes color
from brown to green.
Dandelions **bloom**.

11

Stems poke above the ground. Flowers begin to bloom.

Farmers **plow** the soil and plant seeds.

Spring wakes up animals that **hibernate** all winter. Hungry bears crawl out of their dens to find food.

Frogs swim up from the muddy bottoms of ponds. Snakes leave their winter shelters.

Other animals **migrate** in spring. Birds fly north to build nests and lay eggs.

Whales swim north to feed in colder waters.

Animals give birth to their young in spring. Deer have fawns. Sheep have lambs.

Ducklings and **tadpoles** hatch from eggs.

Spring days are good for flying a kite, playing baseball, or planting a garden.

Spring days grow warmer
and warmer. Soon it will
be summer.

Glossary

bloom—when a flower grows and opens

ducklings—baby ducks

hibernate—to spend the winter in a deep sleep

migrate—to move from one place to another; some animals migrate in the spring and fall.

plow—to turn over the soil; farmers plow the soil to prepare it for planting seeds.

season—one of the four parts of the year; the seasons are spring, summer, fall, and winter.

stem—the main part of a plant; leaves and flowers grow from the stem.

tadpole—a young frog or toad

To Learn More

AT THE LIBRARY
Chall, Marsha Wilson. *Sugarbush Spring.* New York: Lothrop, Lee & Shepard, 2000.

Gibbons, Gail. *The Reasons for Seasons.* New York: Holiday House, 1995.

Jackson, Ellen. *The Spring Equinox: Celebrating the Greening of the Earth.* Brookfield, Conn.: Millbrook Press, 2002.

Rockwell, Anne. *Four Seasons Make a Year.* New York: Walker, 2004.

Shannon, George. *Spring: A Haiku Story.* New York: Greenwillow Books, 1996.

ON THE WEB
Learning more about the seasons is as easy as 1, 2, 3.

1. Go to www.factsurfer.com

2. Enter "seasons" into search box.

3. Click the "Surf" button and you will see a list of related web sites.

With factsurfer.com, finding more information is just a click away.

Index

animals, 14, 16, 18

baseball, 20

bears, 14

birds, 16

deer, 18

ducklings, 19

Earth, 4

eggs, 16, 19

farmers, 13

fawns, 18

flowers, 12

frogs, 15

garden, 20

grass, 11

hibernate, 14

ice, 7

kite, 20

lakes, 7

lambs, 18

leaves, 10

migrate, 16

nests, 16

plants, 10

ponds, 7, 15

rain, 9, 10

seeds, 13

sheep, 18

snakes, 15

snow, 7

soil, 13

stems, 12

summer, 21

sun, 5, 6, 10

tadpoles, 19

thunderstorms, 8

trees, 10

whales, 17

wind, 8

winter, 4, 14, 15

The photographs in this book are reproduced through the courtesy of: Juan Martinez, front cover; Darrell Gulin/Getty Images, pp. 4-5; Hironori Okamoto/Getty Images, p. 5; Adam Jones/Getty Images, p. 6; Frank Krahmer/Getty Images, pp. 7, 10-11; Pete Turner/Getty Images, pp. 8-9; Richard Nebesky/Getty Images, p. 10; Martin Ruegner/Getty Images, p. 12; Chris Close/Getty Images, p. 13; Paul McCormick/Getty Images, p. 14; Caroline von Tuempling/Getty Images, p. 15; Richard Schultz/Getty Images, p. 16; Photolibrarycom/Getty Images, p. 17; Tom Tietz/Getty Images, p. 18; Michael S. Quinton/Getty Images, p. 19; Jim Cummins/Getty Images, p. 20-21.